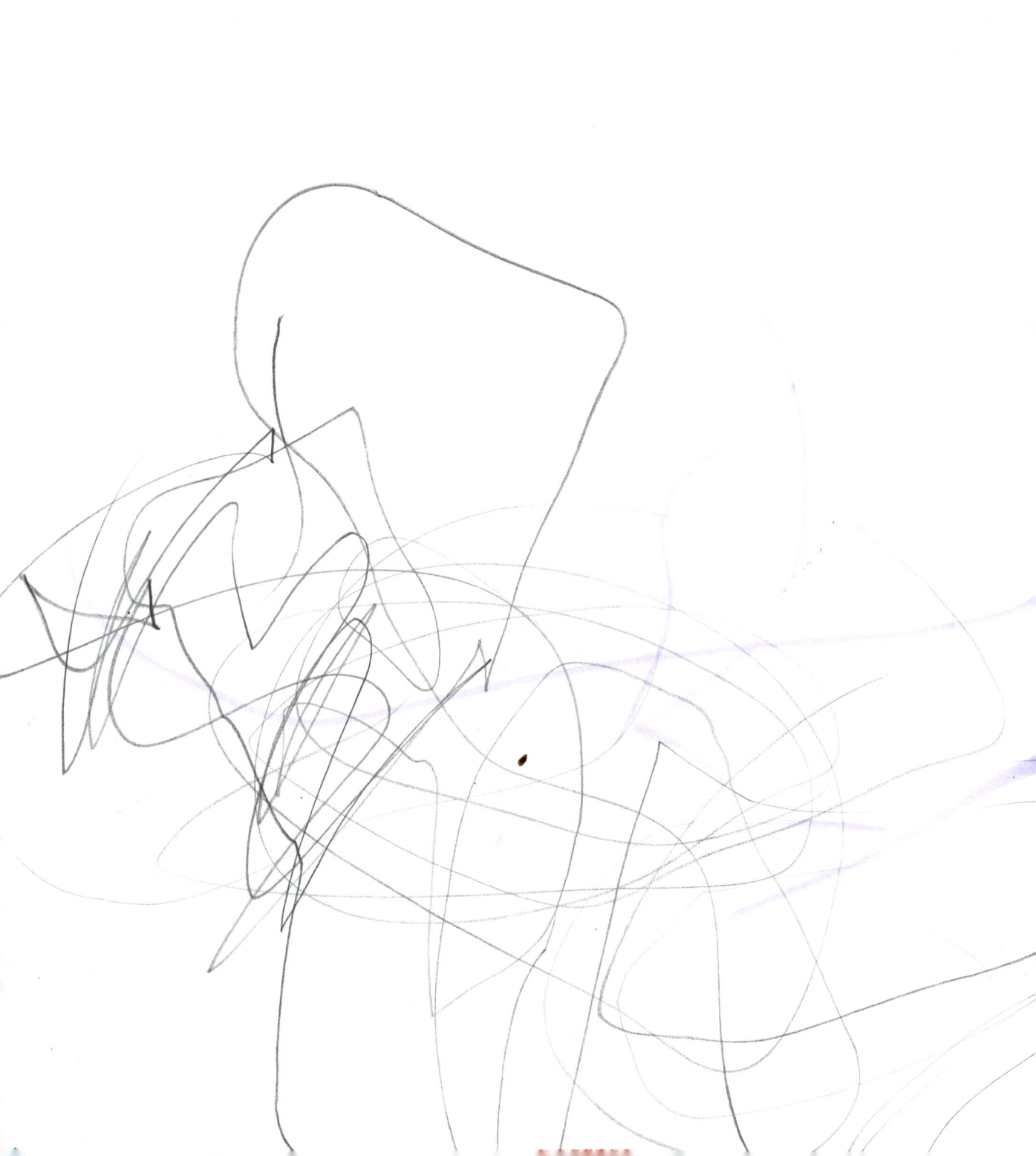

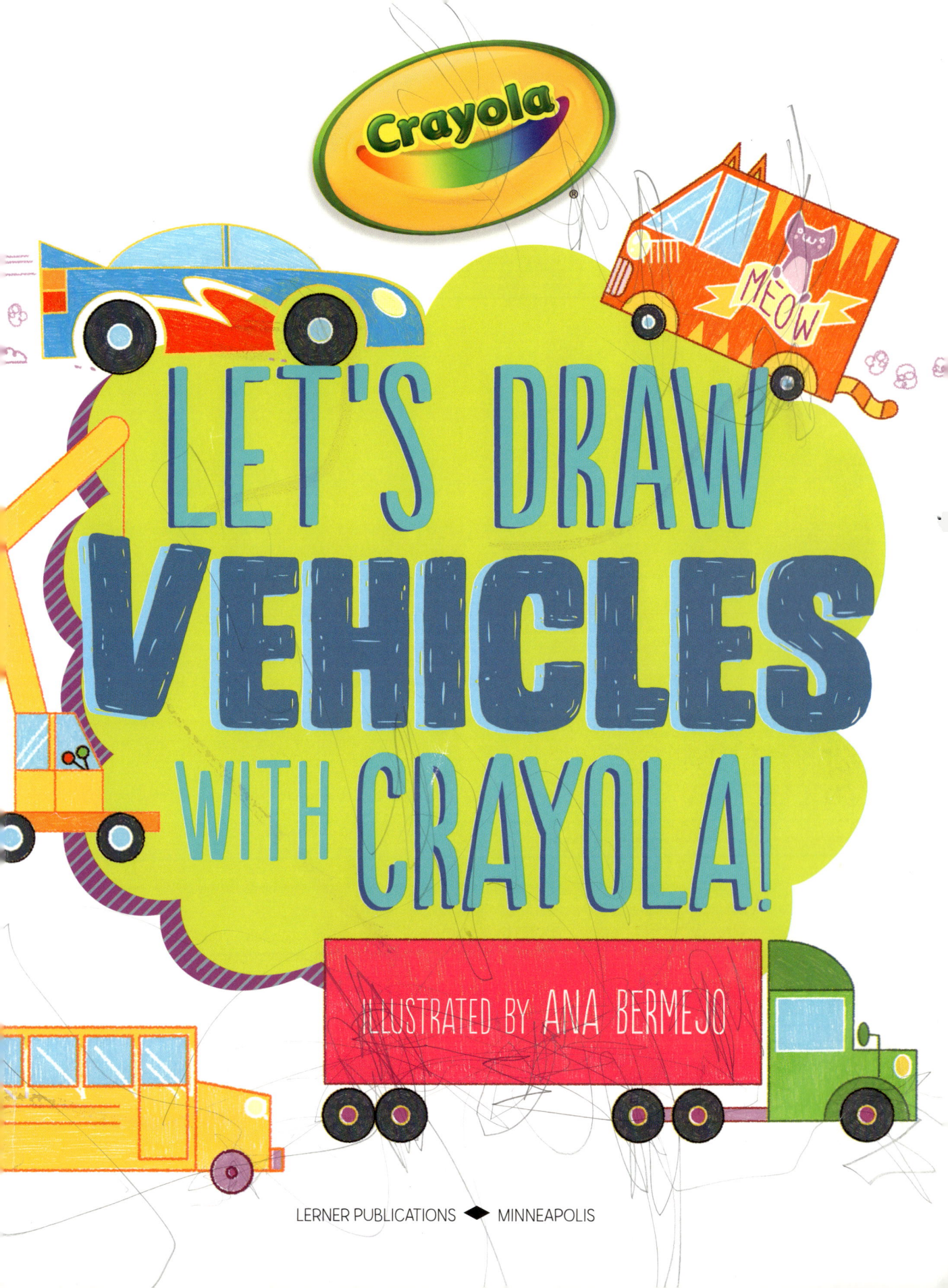

Copyright © 2018 by Lerner Publishing Group, Inc.

All rights reserved. International copyright secured. No part of this book may be reproduced, stored in a retrieval system, or transmitted in any form or by any means—electronic, mechanical, photocopying, recording, or otherwise—without the prior written permission of Lerner Publishing Group, Inc., except for the inclusion of brief quotations in an acknowledged review.

© 2018 Crayola, Easton, PA 18044-0431. Crayola Oval Logo, Serpentine Design, Razzmatazz, Radical Red, Jazzberry Jam, Mango Tango, Vivid Tangerine, Screamin' Green, Manatee, and Wisteria are registered trademarks of Crayola used under license.

Official Licensed Product
Lerner Publications Company
A division of Lerner Publishing Group, Inc.
241 First Avenue North
Minneapolis, MN 55401 USA

For reading levels and more information, look up this title at www.lernerbooks.com.

Main body text set in Billy Infant Regular 24/30.
Typeface provided by SparkyType.

Library of Congress Cataloging-in-Publication Data

Names: Bermejo, Ana, 1978– illustrator.
Title: Let's Draw Vehicles with Crayola®! / illustrated by Ana Bermejo.
Description: Minneapolis : Lerner Publications, 2018. | Series: Let's Draw with Crayola®! | Includes bibliographical references. | Audience: Ages 4-9. | Audience: K to Grade 3. | Description based on print version record and CIP data provided by publisher; resource not viewed.
Identifiers: LCCN 2017011956 (print) | LCCN 2017018542 (ebook) | ISBN 9781512497793 (eb pdf) | ISBN 9781512432978 (lb : alk. paper)
Subjects: LCSH: Motor vehicles in art—Juvenile literature. | Drawing—Technique—Juvenile literature.
Classification: LCC NC825.M64 (ebook) | LCC NC825.M64 D73 2018 (print) | DDC 743/.8962922—dc23

LC record available at https://lccn.loc.gov/2017011956

Manufactured in the United States of America
1-41828-23788-8/25/2017

CONTENTS

Can You Draw Vehicles?......... 4
Cars............................ 6
Trucks......................... 8
Motorcycles................... 10
Trains......................... 12
Race Cars..................... 14
Big Rides..................... 16
Construction Vehicles......... 18
Rescue Vehicles............... 20
Mighty Monster Trucks........ 22
Military Vehicles.............. 24
Space Vehicles................ 26
Zoom City..................... 28

World of Colors.................... 30
To Learn More..................... 32

CAN YOU DRAW VEHICLES?

You can if you can draw shapes! Use the shapes in the box at the top of each page to draw the vehicles. Put vehicle parts together in your drawing to make a fierce military vehicle or a huge monster truck. Or, use the parts to create your own vehicle!

Shapes you will use:
square   triangle   circle   rectangle

···

Wheels

Wipers

Mirrors and Lights

Grilles and Plates

5

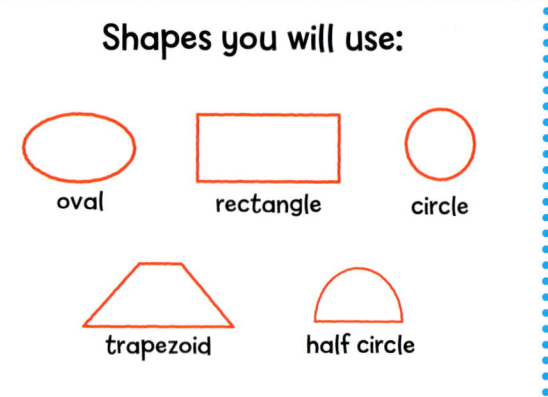

Bugsy

Waggin' Wagon

Convertible

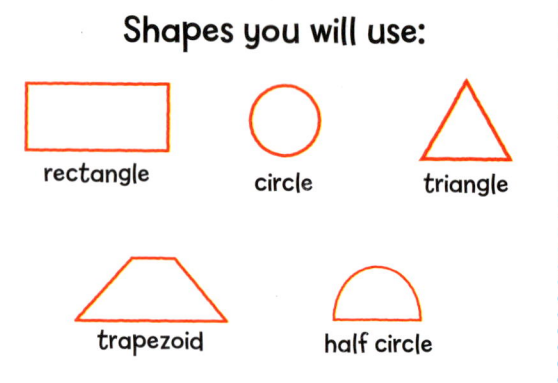

Pickup

Delivery Truck

Meow Mobile

MOTORCYCLES

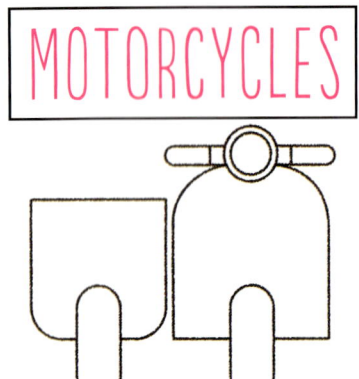

Shapes you will use:

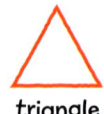

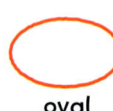

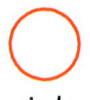

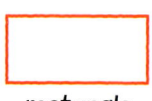

triangle
oval
circle
rectangle

Moped

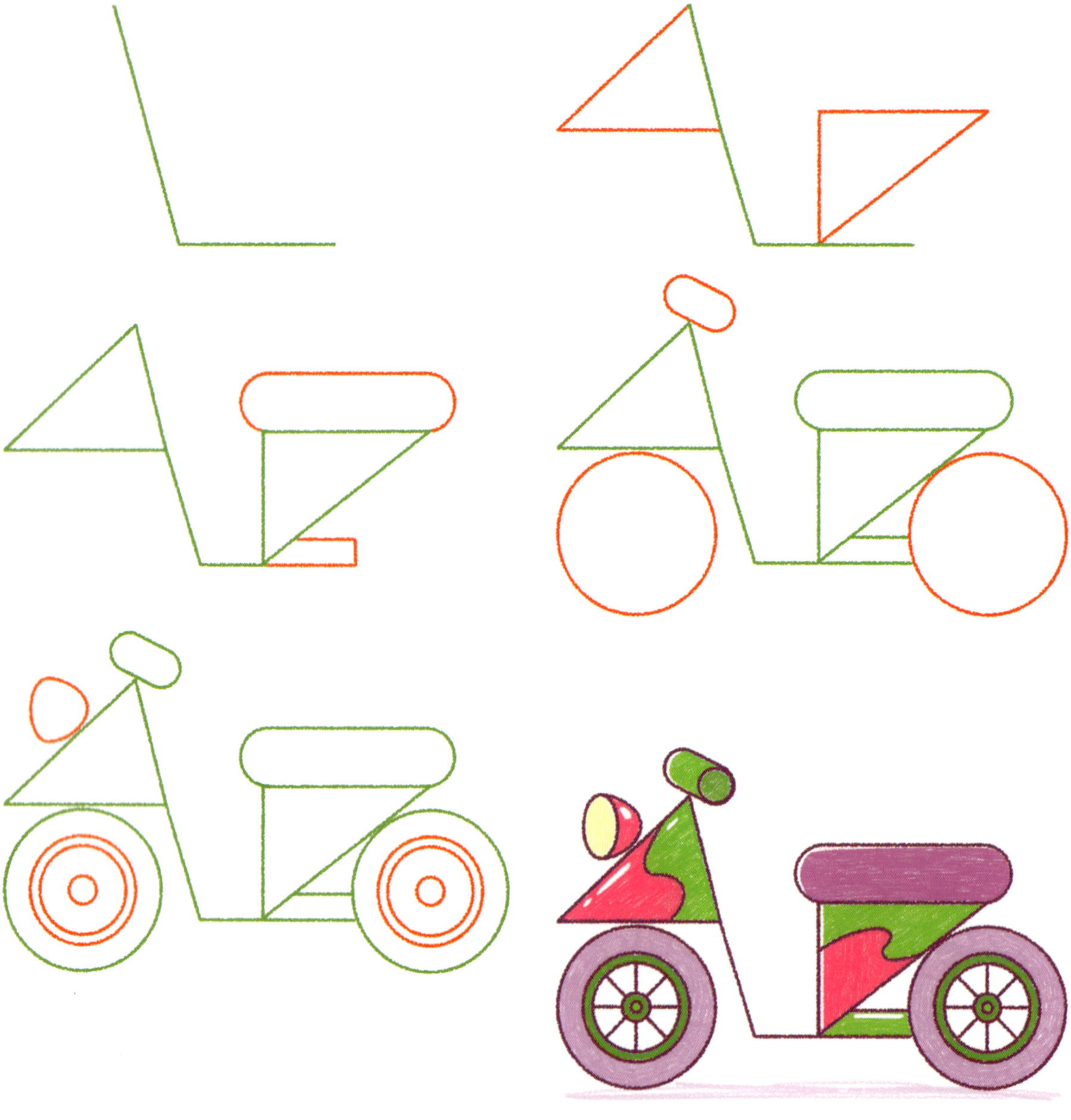

Chopper

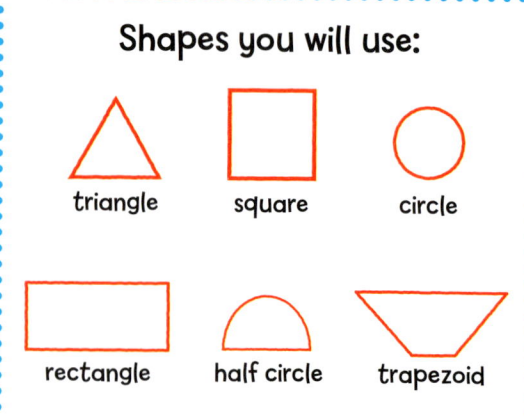

Choo Choo

12

Caboose

Tram

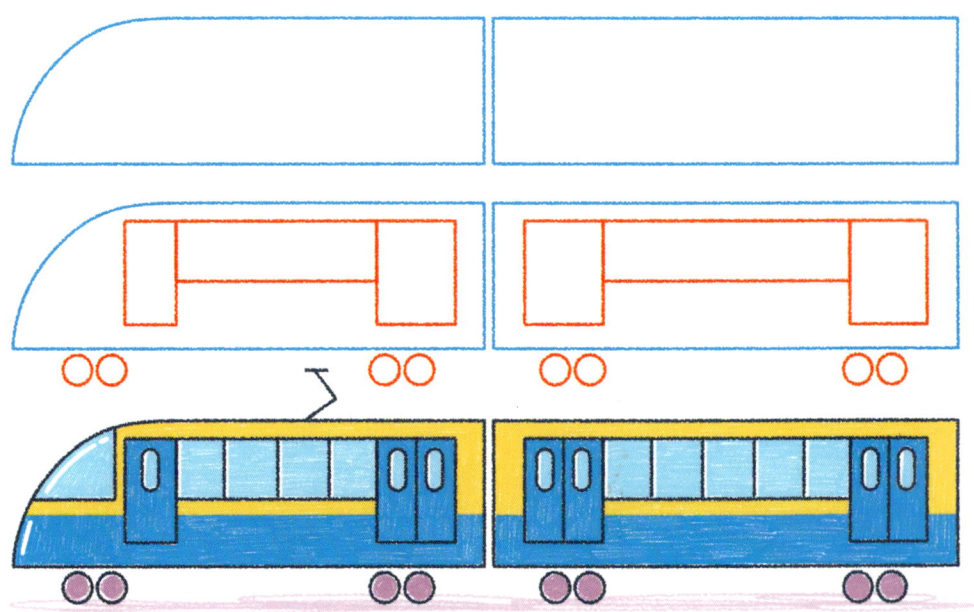

13

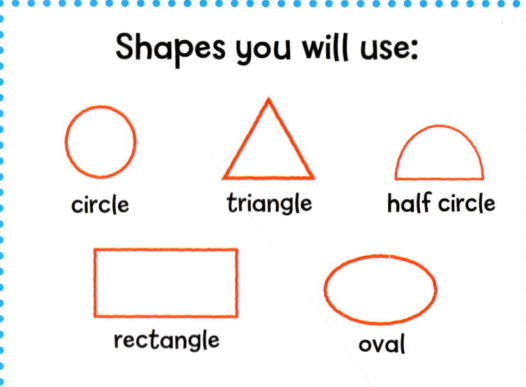

Speedster

Lightning

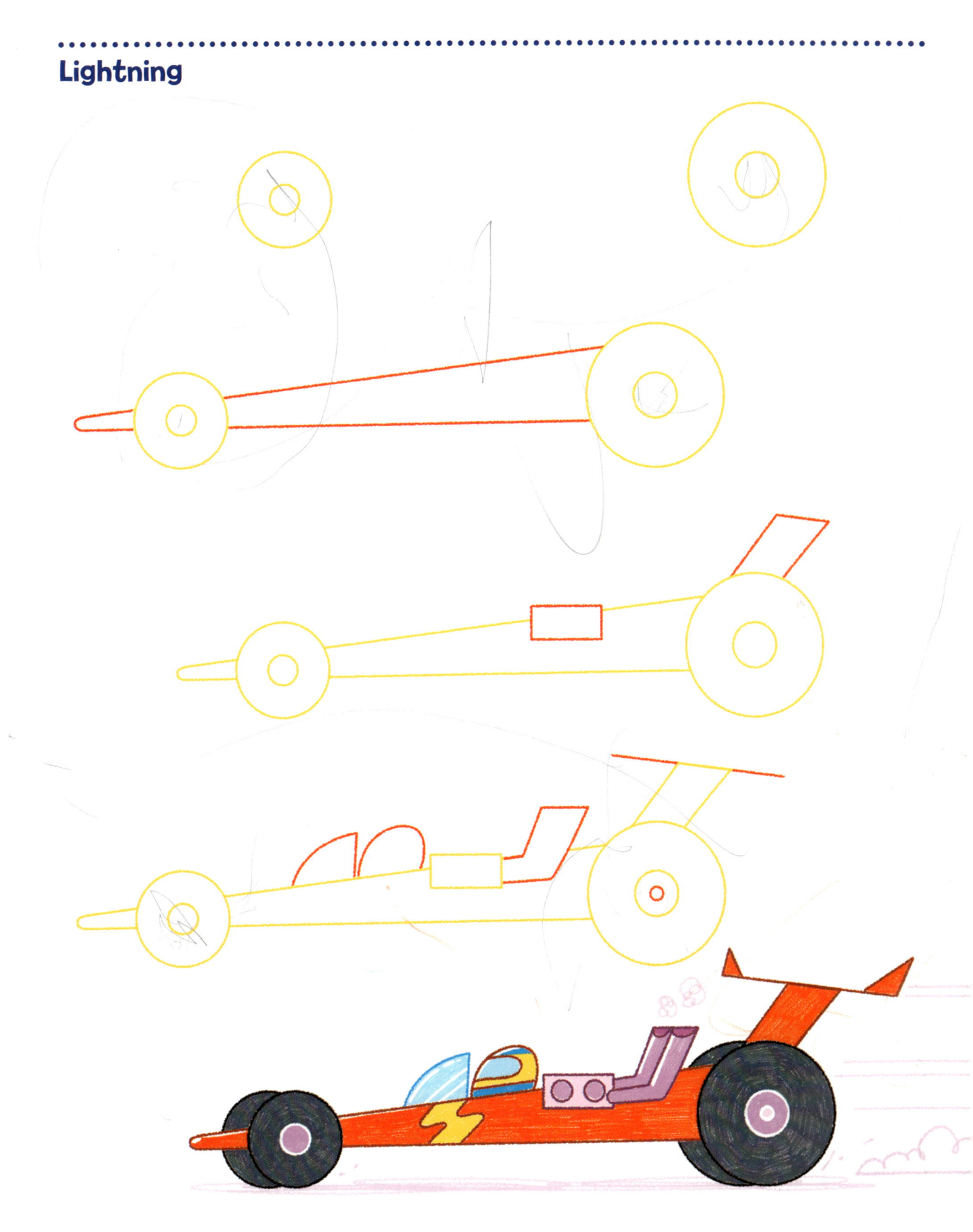

Shapes you will use:

  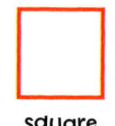

rectangle   circle   square

Cake Delivery!

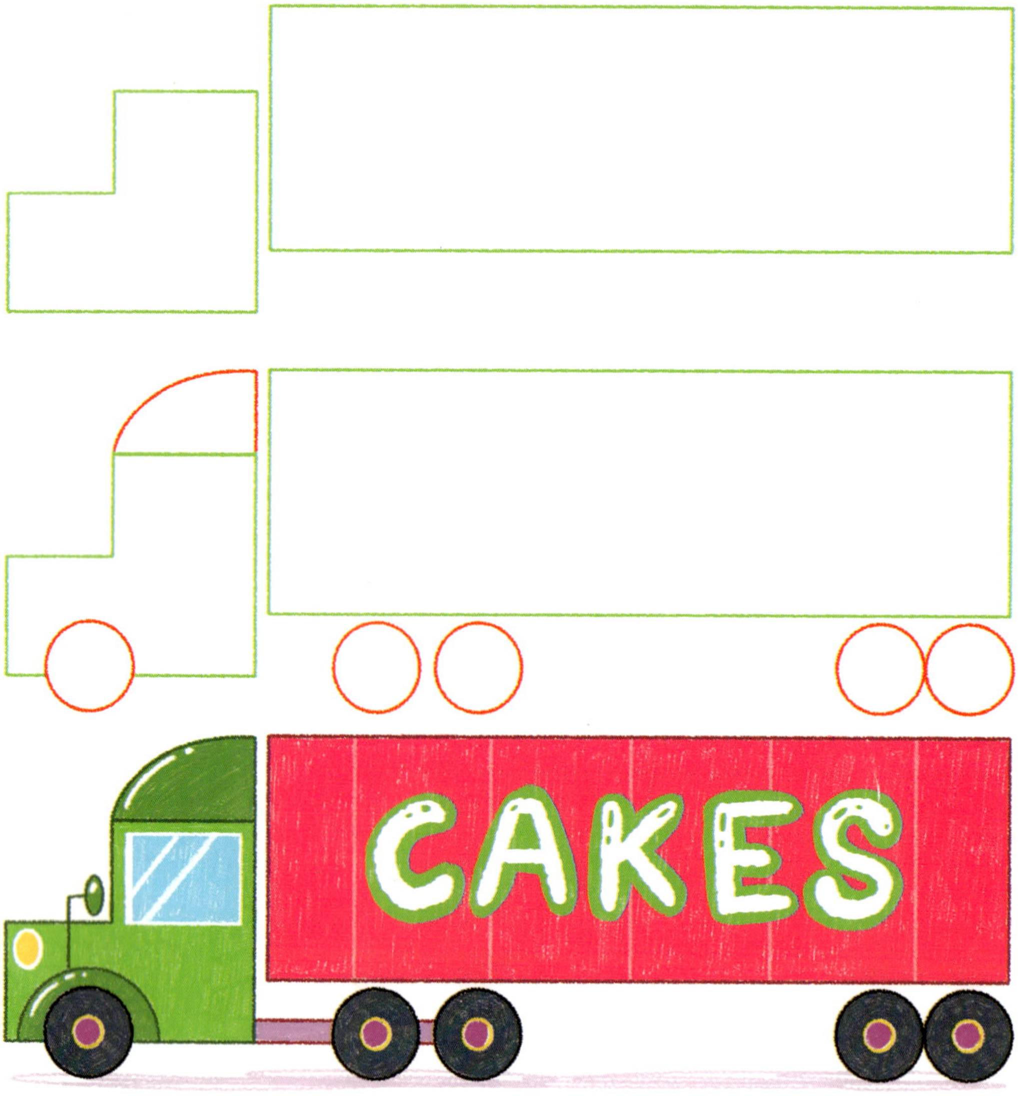

16

Moving Truck

School Bus

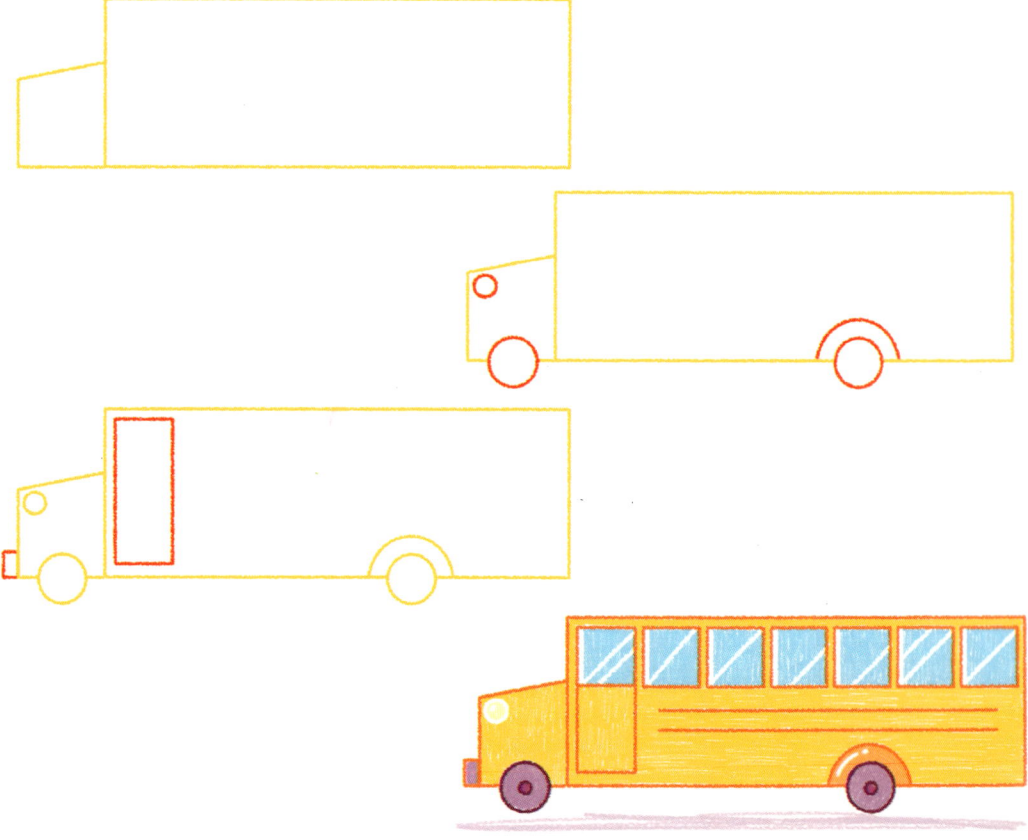

CONSTRUCTION VEHICLES

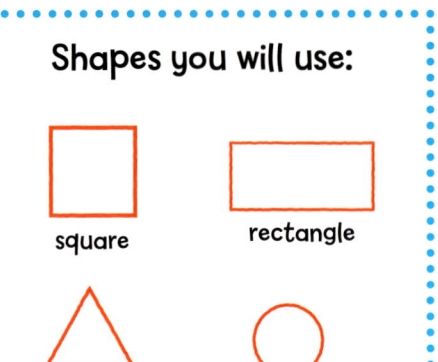

Shapes you will use: square, rectangle, triangle, circle

Lifter

18

Dumper

Mixer

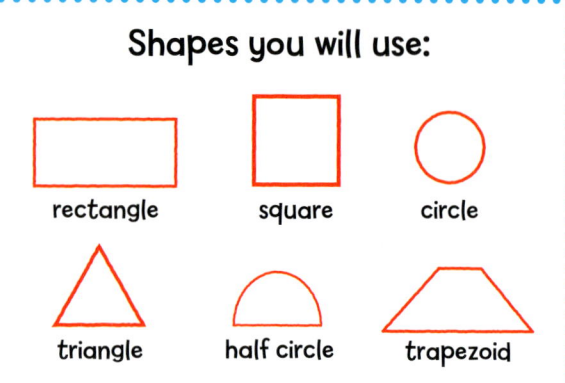

Hook and Ladder

20

HelperCopter

Cruiser

MIGHTY MONSTER TRUCKS

Shapes you will use:

 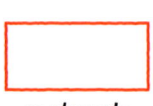  

circle   rectangle   triangle   square

Crusher

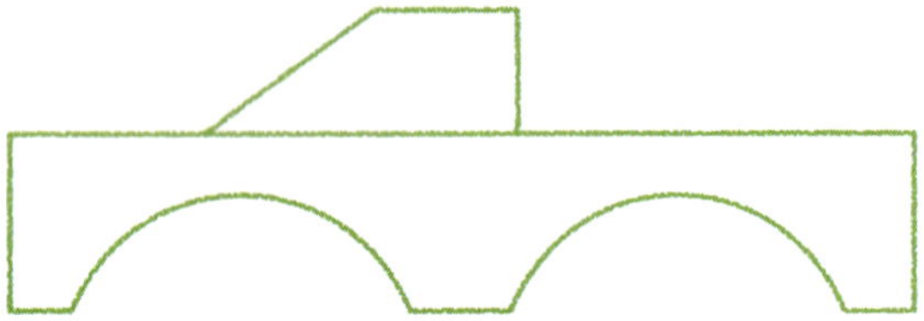

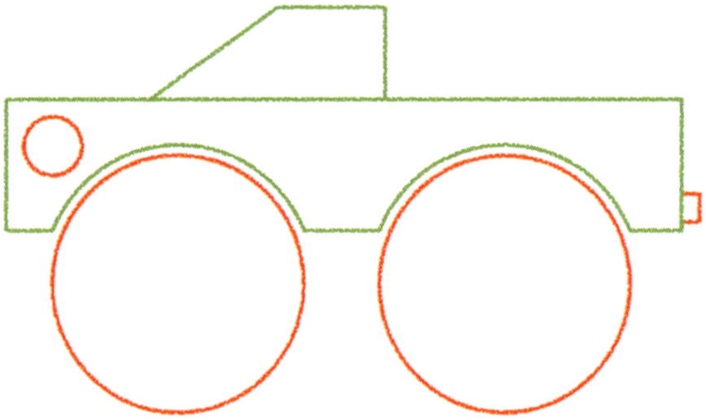

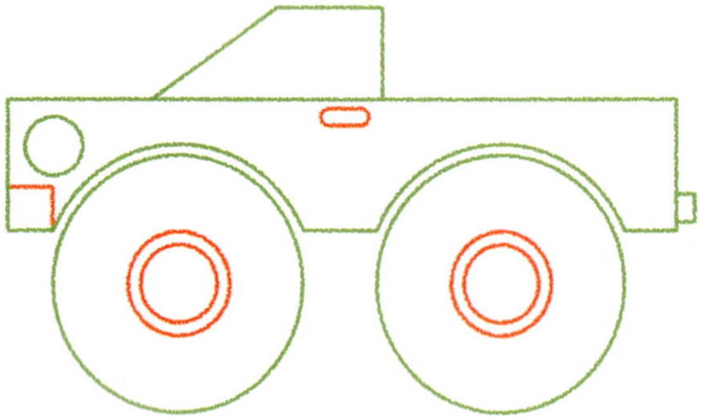

Jaws

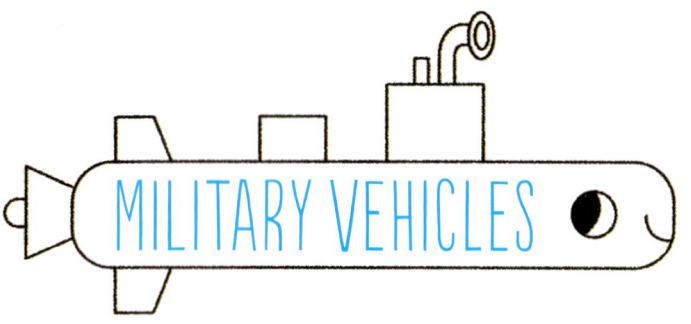

Shapes you will use:

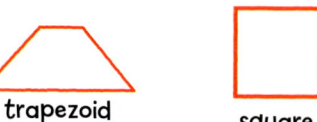

Super Stealth

Subster

SPACE VEHICLES

Shapes you will use:

Rover

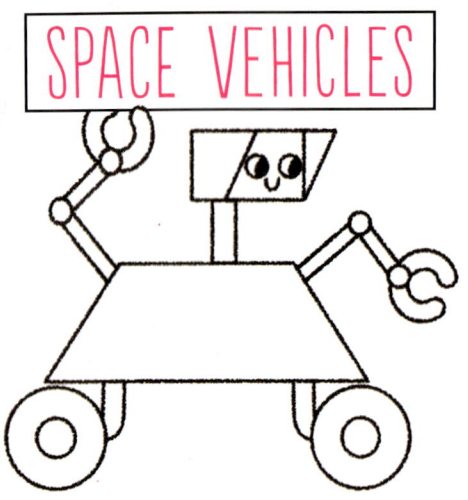

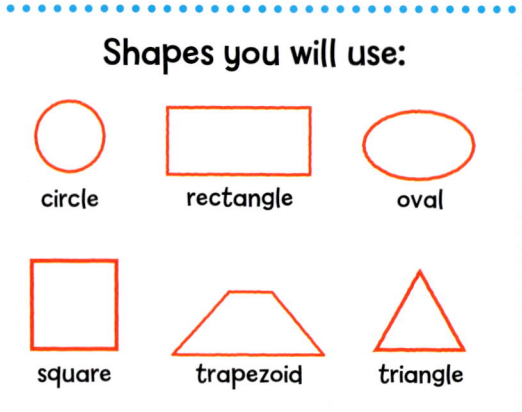

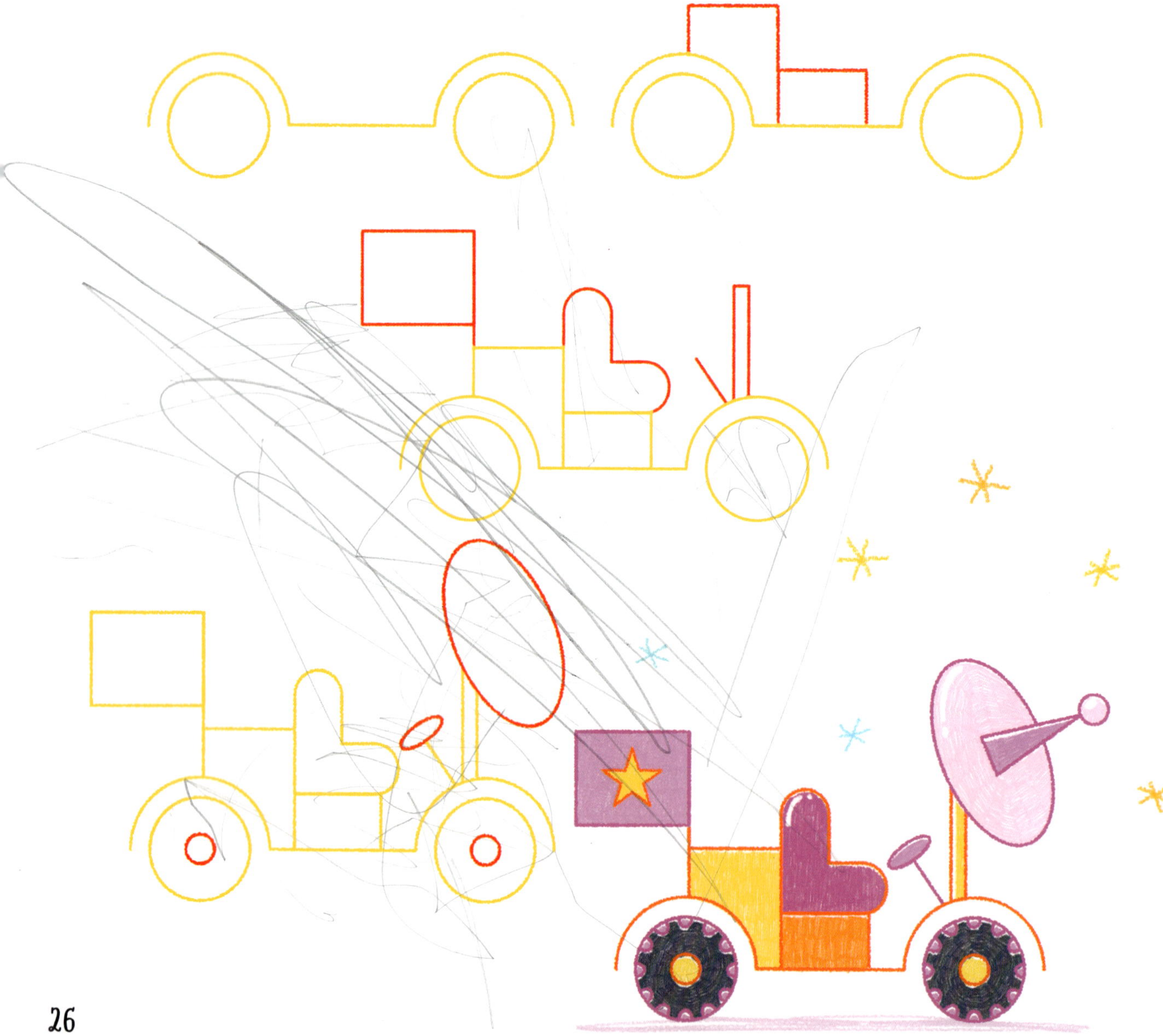

Blastoff

WORLD OF COLORS

Vehicles come in all kinds of colors! Here are some of the Crayola® crayon colors used in this book. What colors will you use to draw your next vehicle?

RAZZMATAZZ • MAROON • RADICAL RED • JAZZBERRY JAM • MANGO TANGO • VIVID TANGERINE • SUNGLOW • YELLOW • GOLDENROD

VROOM! Let's get DRAWING!

GREEN YELLOW · SCREAMIN' GREEN · SHAMROCK · SKY BLUE · TURQUOISE BLUE · BLUE · MANATEE · WISTERIA · ROYAL PURPLE · BLUE VIOLET

31

TO LEARN MORE

Books

Bergin, Mark. *It's Fun to Draw Cars, Planes, and Trains.* New York: Sky Pony, 2015.
Follow the step-by-step instructions of this book to get more practice drawing all kinds of vehicles.

Learn to Draw Cars, Planes & Moving Machines: Step-by-Step Instructions for More Than 25 High-Powered Vehicles. Illustrated by Tom La Padula and Jeff Shelly. Lake Forest, CA: Walter Foster, 2016.
Check out this book to draw even more of your favorite vehicles!

Let's Draw Robots with Crayola! Illustrated by Emily Golden. Minneapolis: Lerner Publications, 2018.
Use this book to learn how to draw flying robots, robot animals, and more.

Websites

Cars
http://www.hellokids.com/r_1963/drawing-for-kids/drawing-tutorials-step-by-step/cars
Visit this website to get more practice drawing cars and other types of vehicles.

Here Comes a Train!
http://www.crayola.com/crafts/here-comes-a-train-craft/
Use your drawing skills to design your own train set, and put your favorite things in each of the cars!